NOT TIME
TO PUT OUT THE LIGHTS

Debbie & Tony

Best Wishes

Stephen

X

NOT TIME

to

PUT OUT THE LIGHTS

MY TRANSPLANT STORY
BILATERAL DOUBLE LUNG TRANSPLANT

Stephen Henstridge

First printed in 2020, reprinted in 2022.

ISBN (Paperback): 978-1-913012-33-5
ISBN (ePub): 978-1-913012-34-2

A full CIP record for this book is available from the British Library.

Published in association with
Riverside Publishing Solutions, Salisbury, UK
www.riversidepublishingsolutions.com

Printed and bound in the UK.

DEDICATION

For Jackie, Sonya and Stuart

For my Donor and her Family

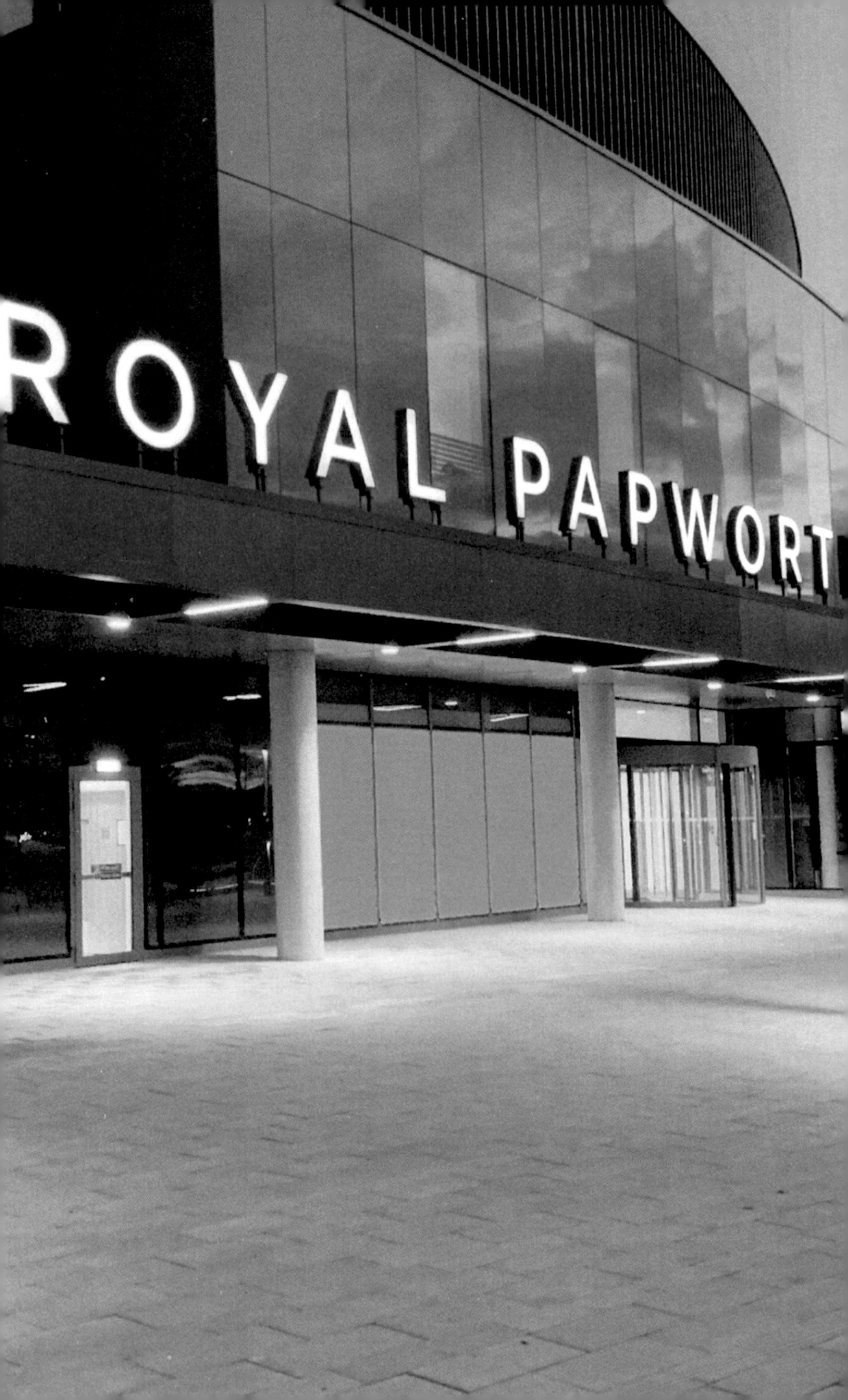
ROYAL PAPWORT

CONTENTS

FOREWORD

I was the first to read Steve's transplant story because I typed it for him. Stephen asked me to read it first before typing it out for him. Even though I had known him for a long time as I am a friend of his wife Jackie, you don't really know the "inner person". To be privy to his innermost thoughts was a real privilege. I think for a man to be so in touch with his emotions is a wonderful thing. I cried and laughed whilst reading his story. It was a real honour to be able to do this small thing for him.

Christine Harding

ABOUT THE AUTHOR

My name is Stephen Henstridge. I am 63 years of age. For all of my working life (47 years) I have worked in the metalwork industry. During my leisure hours I have trained in a gym and kept myself fit for 30 years since finishing playing football. Like most people I enjoy a drink now and then and although I've never smoked cigarettes I did used to enjoy one small cigar with a soft drink whilst sitting on the wall outside of my house each evening, contemplating the events of the day.

I have been married for 40 years to my wonderful wife Jackie who along with my daughter Sonya, and my son Stuart, have been my rock throughout this whole process. I have three grandsons, Reece, Louie and Finley.

INTRODUCTION

The Beginning

I never noticed, or gave any thought to the fact that I was coughing more than usual, mainly because of my busy family life, working and keeping fit, until Jackie and I went on a week's holiday in Derbyshire with Jackie's cousin Liz and her husband Graham. We went out for the day and called in to a farmhouse to have a cup of coffee and a biscuit, and as I went to sit down on a bench outside as I lifted my leg over and flopped down all of a sudden my head started to go numb like, and my vision for a couple of seconds or so went dark, and my hearing had gone, I knew that Jackie and Graham and Liz hadn't noticed anything, so I kept quiet about it, but it really scared me, so when we got back to Graham and Liz's house in Buxton I told Jackie what had happened. She said it could be something really serious and I should go to our GP as soon as we get home for a check-up.

Of course, I told her not to be silly, it was nothing, my fitness from my training would keep me healthy, but after Jackie's constant nagging, I agreed to go to my GP in about June 2014. From there I was referred to a consultant at Salisbury District Hospital and then, after some tests and X-rays, was referred to a much bigger unit for chest related illnesses at Southampton General Hospital.

My first appointment at Southampton Hospital was with a consultant respiratory physician called Doctor Sophie Fletcher, a lovely lady, and after having numerous blood tests and other appointments with her she was unable to diagnose precisely what was wrong with me, so then referred me on to a surgeon, a Mr Amer.

Jackie and I walked into the consultant's room for my appointment with Mr Amer. "Come in and sit down" he said, whilst looking at my scan results on his screen. At this time, I was still training at the gym three times a week, was very strong and still felt really good apart from my cough. The next words Mr Amer said to me shattered my world. "Stephen, this is the worst scarring of the lungs that I have ever seen in a man of your age (which at that time was 59). This disease is usually found in older people, say between 65 to 70 year olds, and for you to be this bad at your age is really unusual".

Well, I was looking at the consultant thinking "you what? What the hell are you talking about, you can't be right what with all the training I do and everything". I still felt really good in myself, but he knew what was around the corner for me.

On July 24th, 2016, I had a lung biopsy operation in Southampton to try and help diagnose my condition. On my next appointment at Southampton hospital I was told that I had Idiopathic Pulmonary Fibrosis (IPF), a serious life-threatening disease which has no cure.

Idiopathic means that there is no known cause as to why I have this condition.

Jackie and I walked out of the hospital with coffee and sandwiches and sat on a bench and tried to digest the fact that I was terminally ill, with no known time limit because this disease affects different people in various time frames.

Over the next year and a half my lung function gradually got worse until I reached a level by which I qualified for a relatively new drug.

I was then prescribed a drug called Nintedanib, a specialist new drug to help slow up the symptoms of

IPF, such as breathlessness etc., but after about two years I was still getting worse so on my next appointment at Southampton Hospital my consultant said she thought it a good idea that we should think about a lung transplant. This again was a shock, but I was referred to the Royal Papworth Hospital for tests to see if I was a suitable candidate for a transplant.

I was accepted and put on to a lung clinic list (not live) but, after several more appointments, in March 2019 I was officially put on a live transplant waiting list. I cannot begin to tell you how it feels to know that from then on I had to have my phone with me at all times, my bag packed ready at home and to not be more than about one hour away from my home at all times. To start with I felt very on edge, almost jumpy and nervous, constantly wondering when the call would come but after a few days, then weeks, I gradually learnt to adapt and just be patient and wait for that call. Whilst I was on the live list one thing did keep occurring in my thoughts – I wondered who was out there now, living their life like any normal person, who would eventually become part of me because of their kindness in being a donor. It really makes you think again about everything in your life.

SUNDAY MAY 5th, 2019

First Call

At approximately 7.15am I was woken by my phone ringing. Startled, I answered, and it was Papworth. Could I be ready in an hour when an ambulance would be here to take me to hospital as they think they have a match for me. (Always the patient is called and taken to the hospital first, that way if it goes ahead then the patient is in position). Jackie and I panicked a little, but we had everything ready and in order. My head was buzzing, thoughts everywhere. Jackie was making phone calls to the family.

The ambulance came and we eventually arrived at Papworth where Jackie and I were taken to my own room. Sonya and Stuart were following in Stuart's car and they were about an hour behind us. I was seen in my room by a transplant specialist nurse, given my gown and told to have a shower and then await developments as they happened. As you can imagine, time then seems to just hang and whilst waiting for news I was getting more and more nervous. I was tired and not talking much but wondering in my mind if this was the day.

At about 4.00pm the nurse came into my room and brought the news that the donor lungs were not good enough, so I had to get dressed and we made our way back home. At this point I didn't really know if I was relieved or disappointed, but I did know that I would be a little bit better prepared for the next time, if I was called again.

On the way home I sat quietly in the back of Stu's car with Jackie by my side. I kept thinking about what might have been, all of the information I had read in the different booklets about transplants that Papworth give you to help you understand the procedures and possible risks involved were all going through my head. I felt tired and drained and think I had an hour's sleep or so before we arrived home. Of course, when we got home Jackie had to start ringing everyone that she had rang earlier that morning telling them I had been called, to tell everything was called off. It was very disappointing for all of my family and friends as well; these things affect so many people in different ways.

I should also point out that at this time I was using liquid oxygen which had been prescribed to me during a lung rehabilitation programme that Papworth wanted me to attend at Salisbury District Hospital. During exercise, the physiotherapy team noticed that my oxygen levels were dangerously low and so therefore I had to start using liquid oxygen.

I think in truth I was in denial about needing this, what with my belief in my fitness from the 28 years of gym training, but unbeknown to me even my friends who I had trained with at the gym for years had noticed how I was struggling with my training, doing less, coughing more and taking longer breaks between my sets of exercise. This was all in 2018, about a year before my transplant.

I was also still working four days a week, having given up working on Mondays because I had got used to having them off to attend the lung programme at the hospital. It would have been quite easy for me to have stopped working permanently at this time, but the way I saw it was that if I could keep myself at a certain level of fitness, and try to keep living my life as normally as possible (and that included going to work) then this would all give me a better chance of coming through this whole process. I think that my friends all noticed how much I was sliding downwards but no one wanted to tell me in case the truth would hurt me, but I already knew in my heart that I was now at the point where I really did want my phone to ring.

WEDNESDAY 29th MAY 2019

Second Call

And ring it did at about 9.00am. The phone went and the same procedure started all over again, but this time we weren't so panicked, but the same feelings were flooding through my system. The ambulance arrived and within the hour we were on our way to Papworth again. Luckily for me I had already eaten a light breakfast, because once I had taken the call, I was only allowed water until told otherwise. The journey was going very well, and I was more relaxed this time. After travelling about 130 miles the ambulance driver's phone rang and he was told to pull over at the next lay-by and ring Papworth then hand the phone over to me. He did as they asked and when I spoke to the transplant coordinator they were desperately sorry to have to tell me that the donor lungs had already been ruled out and that we should turn around and head back home.

This was devastating news as we were only 15 miles from Papworth, but we had no choice. Jackie was upset and crying so I tried to comfort her. I think that this whole process is sometimes harder for all your loved ones and family than it is for the person facing the transplant.

We arrived home, thanked the ambulance driver and went in and put the kettle on for a cup of tea. Then we sat quietly and just tried to take in the events of the day.

For the next few months, we just lived by the rules, always ready, me watching my weight (about 80kg) and trying to keep myself as well and fit as I could at the time. There was one more regular appointment at Papworth during this time and I did have to tell them that I had started to cough up some blood when my cough was at its worst, although it didn't happen every time I coughed. It was another sign that I was getting much worse.

Summer came and summer went and before we knew it, autumn was upon us.

WEDNESDAY 25th SEPTEMBER, 2019

Third Call

As usual I was at work when my phone rang at about 3.45pm. I quickly grabbed it from the top pocket of my overalls and answered the call. It was from the transplant coordinator at Papworth, who was a lovely lady called Sadie.

She asked, "is that Stephen"?

I replied "yes, it is".

"Can you be home within the hour because we think we have a match for you and there will be an ambulance coming to pick you up in an hour".

"Yes, I will be waiting".

"Have you had anything to eat since lunchtime?"

"No, I haven't eaten since 1.00pm."

"Good, don't eat or drink anything except water until you get to the hospital where I will meet you on your arrival."

I then ran into the office and asked the secretary to ring Jackie to let her know an ambulance was on its way for us. I then went and calmly told the news to a couple of my work mates before getting changed to drive back home.

My feelings were different this time. I somehow knew deep inside that this was the day that my life was going to change forever. On the drive home, alone in my car, I had to keep talking out loud to myself, telling myself to be calm and to not panic. Because of the time of the call I knew that we would be arriving at Papworth early in the evening and that most major transplants usually happen overnight, so I thought that this was all pointing to this happening tonight although, of course nothing, is guaranteed.

When I arrived home, I jumped in the shower while Jackie got my things ready and then the ambulance arrived, a BMW X5 and the driver's name was Dan. He asked Jackie if she would like to travel with us or wait and come up with Stuart and Sonya because we were going to be blue lighted with sirens all the way as I had to get to Papworth as soon as possible. Jackie opted to come with us, so Dan strapped her in the rear seat and I was in the passenger seat with my oxygen on.

I was really nervous by now, almost shaking if that's the right word, again my mind was working overtime, I was trying to keep calm and reassure myself that everything was going to be OK.

The journey to Papworth from our house usually takes about two and a half hours. We left our house at 5.00pm and arrived at Papworth at 6.35pm. It was a journey I will never forget, so quick, everything almost blurred. Jackie and the driver Dan were sometimes trying to talk to me but although I was listening, I wasn't really taking anything in.

Once we arrived at Papworth Dan went into the hospital to get a wheelchair to take me in. I said I could walk but he said no, I was to go in the chair. Jackie carried my bag and I remember looking at the sky, by now it was starting to get really dusky and it was quite chilly and the thought went through my head that this could be the last time I would ever see this. I didn't say anything to Jackie because I didn't want to upset her. I tried to keep my thoughts to myself because all of these different thoughts only last for a few seconds before you move on to think of something else, and I wondered if I had done everything I had planned to do while I was waiting for the call, and the answer was no.

I hadn't put pen to paper and written down the things I should have. Of course, my family know that I love them all dearly but it's not the same as writing down on paper to each one of them what I wanted to say, something that they could have and keep in the event that things didn't work out. I am not normally a negative person, my glass is always half full, but you have to face reality when faced with the huge events that me and my family were about to face. It was negligent of me not to have done this, and although I told myself things were going to work out, I really regret not doing what I had intended.

Dan wheeled me to the reception desk. The lady was expecting us and gave us the level and room number we were to go to. We got into the lift and when we arrived at our level and made our way to my room, Sadie was waiting for us. It was reassuring to see her, you could tell that she had been here many times before, her confidence in her work and her ability to talk and to calm us and start my procedures off.

The time was now about 7.45pm. Again, I had my weight, blood pressure and height checked before having a shower in a special solution to kill any bacteria on my body, then it was into my gown and onto the bed. Sonya and Stuart had now arrived and the four of us were nervously awaiting further developments. It's funny sometimes, I was with the woman I love and have spent 44 years with, my two children Sonya, who is 38 and Stuart who is 34, yet it felt that I was almost a stranger, locked away in my thoughts more and more as the minutes ticked by.

One thing I did think about was the loss of my Mum three years earlier to a lung disease very closely related to mine, because I do have a belief and I did ask for guidance from above and I said a prayer to myself and asked in it that my Mum be by my side this night. This may seem strange for a man of 62 but these thoughts, and the fact that my family were all with me to support me, meant that I could finally start to wind down and prepare myself for my miracle.

As the minutes ticked by Sadie came to see us to keep us updated on the progress of the donor lungs. The fact that it was now about 10.30pm and we hadn't been sent home made us even surer it was going to happen. I could sense as the time went by now how tired, almost worn down, we had all become, me looking at Jackie and the kids and thinking that I'd hoped I'd been a good Dad and husband, but it gave me strength to know that we were a very close family and the three of them would have each other, to help and support each other while events unfolded.

It was about 11.45pm, the door was opened and in came Sadie. She was about to say the words that I will never forget, almost as if they are imprinted in my mind:

"Stephen, everything is go, the lungs are good and they are here."

I was almost stunned and I almost didn't believe what she was saying but before I could react Sadie came over to me with what looked like large capsules in silver foil, and told me to take them as they were the first dose of anti-immunosuppressants which would help my body to accept the new lungs. With that done Sadie told me she would be back in a minute to wheel me down to theatre. It was like those words were going into my head, but I wasn't really taking them all in, as if this was happening to someone else. I suppose I was a little in shock, but I didn't have much time to think about it too deeply. Sadie came back into the room with a wheelchair and said it was time to go, as the time was now about midnight.

Jackie, Sonya and Stuart walked with us to the line in the operating department which they could not cross. Sadie stopped as now was the time for me to say what I wanted to say to my loved ones. I kissed them and told them I loved them and as it was now time to go the last thing I did was hold Jackie's hand, kiss her again and said to her to please to not worry (stupid thing to say) and I would see her around. Why I said those words, I'll never know, but I think they come from a song that I love called "I'll be around" by the Spinners. Sadie asked if I was ready, I nodded because if I had tried to speak I would have broken down, and the last thing I wanted was for my family to see me upset or think that I was scared because I wasn't scared, it was just that my mind was all over the place now.

One thing that did stick in my mind was what Sadie said to us en route to the operating area. She told us that that night my surgeon was Mr Steven Tsui, and if there was one surgeon who she would have to transplant her lungs it would be him. This, coming from the transplant coordinator senior nurse gave me real hope and peace of mind. Sadie pushed me off the line and as we headed for the operating theatre, which was about 20 metres or so away I remember looking back round over my left shoulder and seeing Sonya and Stuart either side of Jackie just about to go around the corner out of the unit. Please turn around just one more time I thought, one last look at your faces, but in the blink of an eye they were gone.

I turned back around and we were at the entrance of the operating theatre. As Sadie pushed me into theatre, I remember thinking how space aged everything looked. I could see the table and the giant lights above it, all the equipment, screens, tubes and lines and I thought of the hours that lay ahead, I could see myself on the table being operated on. As we approached the table I remember seeing about three or four people in their scrubs, and as I looked to my right I could see in to what looked like a wash room and there were, I think, three surgeons washing their arms and hands with what looked like caps on their heads and I thought that must be Mr Tsui and his team. Sadie stopped at the operating table her job done. I think she wished me luck before leaving.

I felt cold and alone, although I wasn't of course, and the anaesthetist said "hi Steve, would you like to get up onto the operating table" so I did. I led down on my back with my head on a pillow, I was a bit shivery now and a theatre nurse came over to me and held my hand and asked if I would like a blanket, I said I would so she got one and wrapped it around me. My mind was wandering again now, but I can't remember what I was thinking about. The next thing I remember was the anaesthetist saying he was going to give me something to relax me before putting me to sleep. I think that the time was now about 12.15am and all of a sudden I remember a slow darkness closing my eyes and that must have been when I was put under.

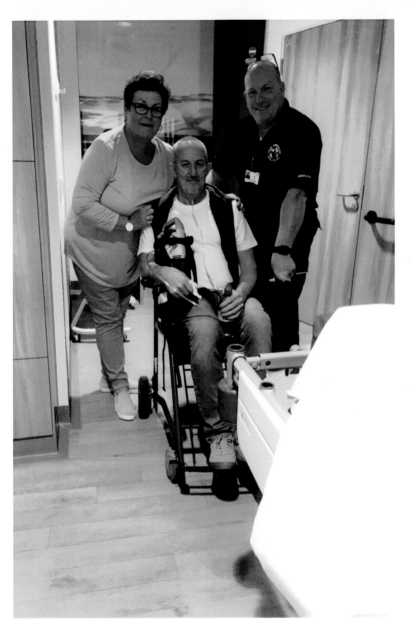

Arriving at Papworth

With Mr Steven Tsui

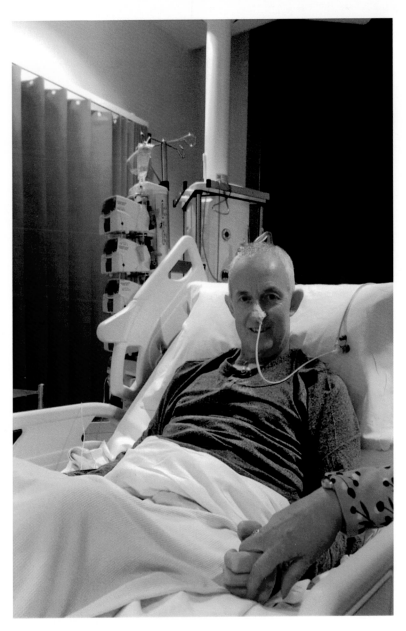

In Critical Care

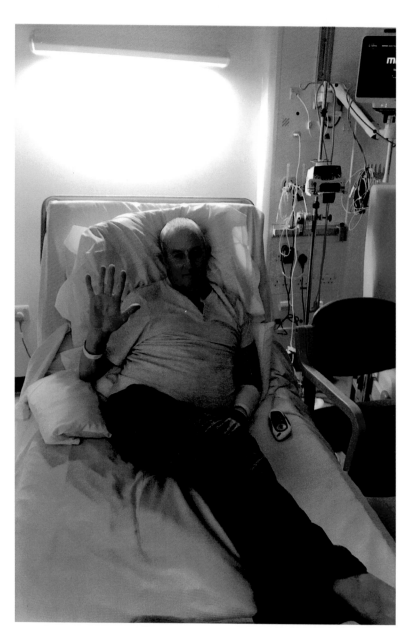

North 5 Recovery

THURSDAY 26th
SEPTEMBER, 2019

Sixteen Hours later – Critical Care

Jackie, Sonya and Stuart were in the Critical Care waiting room, the door opened, and a transplant nurse walked in and said to them that Mr Tsui wanted to see them. They were taken up to the Critical Care level and then had to wait in a room until Mr Tsui came to them. All three of them were dog tired because they had had no sleep the night before and the time was now approximately 5.00pm, some seventeen hours after I went down for my operation.

Mr Tsui entered the room and sat down. He started to explain to the family about my transplant which had taken approximately fifteen and a half hours, a huge amount of time. He said that my operation took a long time as it was very, very difficult and complicated.

He went on to tell Jackie, Sonya and Stuart that he didn't think anyone realised quite how desperate the situation was, and that in his opinion I only had a matter of weeks, maybe a couple of month at best to live, and I was almost past the point of having a transplant and could, and probably would, have been taken off of the transplant list had my call not come when it did. He went on to say that my lungs were in a terrible state, the Fibrosis had scarred the inside of my lungs, making them almost hard, and where this had made them start to shrink this had then caused my diaphragm to rise and my ribcage to gradually pull in, therefore cutting down the space in my chest for my new lungs to fit in to.

My left lung was transplanted first, taking about six hours, and this was carried out with my own body supporting my life systems but the real problems started when my body could not support the right lung transplant and I had to be put on to an ECMO machine. This is a wonderful piece of equipment that is outside of the body and it pumps and oxygenates the blood, thus taking the place of your heart and lungs but it is like having another operation to add to the surgery I was already having. My new lungs were also slightly damaged, due to the time my surgery took and therefore Mr Tsui had to make room in my chest for my new lungs to fit in and this all took time.

Mr Tsui told the family that I was on the edge, critically ill. Jackie asked him if he thought I would survive. He said he really didn't know but they had given me my best chance possible of being able to survive.

I can only imagine the turmoil my family must have gone through that night, wondering how things were going, sleeping or cat napping when they could and just waiting for updates on my progress through the night and then into the next day.

I was now in Bay number 7 in Critical Care where I would be kept for the next six days in an induced coma with the ECMO keeping me alive.

I thank God that my surgeon that night was Mr Steven Tsui and his team, for without their skill and dedication for fifteen and a half hours I would surely be dead. Mr Tsui said to me, when I had been out of my coma for a day or so, that when he visited me when I was still in a coma he came over to me and he touched my shoulder as he spoke to me and said that he felt a certain strength in my body and he was confident that I would survive. He is a wonderful man and I was very touched to hear these words from him.

While I was still in a coma Jackie, Sonya and Stuart visited every day and they told me that they talked to me all the time and that my eyes sometimes flickered as if I could hear them and understand what they were saying but, of course, I don't have any recollection of this.

I think my family made friends with quite a few of the wonderful, dedicated Critical Care nurses who were looking after me whilst I was in a coma. Jackie said to me that it was hard to see me in intensive care with all of those different lines, tubes and the noise of the drivers for the medication going all the time. I think my family became quite expert at looking at the screen that showed all my vital signs and understanding what they meant.

For any family to gain access to the critical care unit you have to go to a waiting room from where you talk via an intercom, and are then allowed into the unit. It was during this time that Jackie, Sonya and Stuart met and became friends with a couple of other families, and this contact proved to be so helpful because the different families could all support and talk and bounce off of each other, whilst myself and their loved ones were in a coma. Donna, whose husband Jimmy had had a double lung transplant like me, and Lizzie, whose partner Sam had a serious lung condition and was in the bay next to mine. The families used to see each other most days and compare notes of their loved ones progress, and this continued throughout the time I was in hospital and still does to this day, I regularly speak to Jimmy on the phone and we compare notes, and Jackie and I have met up with Donna and Jimmy and Lizzie and Sam. The support and friendship at times like these is invaluable in helping your family cope with everything.

I have a very strong and vivid memory of something that happened during a procedure while I was still in a coma. I'm not sure what the procedure was but I remember some sort of commotion and I was in and out of consciousness but all of a sudden I felt a calm like darkness and the feeling that I was falling into a big empty dark void. I thought somehow that this was the end, all the weight seemed to lift from my mind and I remember thinking how peaceful this was when all of a sudden I was being manhandled and then I heard a loud voice saying "we've got to call this." With that a number of staff were around my bed and an oxygen mask was pushed hard onto my face, the man who was at my head with the mask was barking out orders to the other staff around me and taking control. The next thing I remember is being pushed along some corridors and into a lift to be taken up to the CT scanner. This must have showed that I was bleeding internally and that there was a serious number of blood clots in my right upper chest so at this point I think I was rushed back to theatre to have my chest drained. How I can remember this, I don't know, but the next thing I do remember is a voice speaking to me saying "Stephen, its Tuesday 1st October, you've been asleep for nearly six days. Well I can't really say that I understood what was happening, my eyes were opening and then shutting, but finally I must have been woken from my induced coma.

Please remember that this is not a medical account of my transplant, it's only the things I remember. The times are only approximate, but the memories are real and vivid.

Slowly I started to be able to focus, although I was unable to move and I realised that I had tubes everywhere, one up my nose going down into my stomach which was for my food for the next three and a half weeks, and I had a catheter on my front and one behind for my toilet needs. During this time of trying to take everything in, all the different noises on the Critical Care level were to me almost non-stop, the nurses talking and always busy, the different monitors going off all the time, and me just led there as if I was in a different world. At this time I was still breathing with a ventilator and I had a huge and what felt like a solid dressing across my chest, but I don't remember any pain as such.

I was still very tired and weak, but a wonderful moment was when all of a sudden Jackie, Sonya and Stuart came into my view. They tried to get near me to hug and kiss me but of course it was difficult with all of the machines and tubes around me but we managed it and to me it was like being born again, to see them was so emotional.

Jackie reached into her bag and took out a handful of cards sent to me by friends and family, and one in particular made me cry, it was sent by my workmates, they had all signed it wishing me well and a speedy recovery, but there was one message that my friend Matty wrote that he knew that I would know straight away what he meant, the words he wrote were "All the best Hen, (my nickname), not time to put out the lights." We go to a lot of live music events together, and "Put out the Lights" is a track that one of my favourite live bands, The Oyster Band, play and it really made me think of how close I was to my lights going out during my transplant, but here I was able to read those lovely words in Papworth, and I just thought how lucky I was to still be alive. That is why I have given my book the title – NOT TIME TO PUT OUT THE LIGHTS.

But there were hard times ahead for me in critical care. I was not allowed solid food or water, my food was administered by a machine which squeezed a protein substance through the tube in my nose into my stomach and water was totally off limits, in order to keep my new lungs dry. My mouth at times was so dry but I was allowed to bite onto a small sponge on the end of a stick with cold water in it, but I could not swallow it and had to spit it out, but at least it gave me moisture in my mouth.

I could not believe how vulnerable I felt. I could see how much weight I had lost, I didn't even have the strength in my body to lift my arm. When you consider that the night before I was called for my transplant I was in the gym doing my exercises and was really strong considering my illness, yet here I was a week later so weak that I struggled to even move my fingers, and the thought of how my life had changed in that short time really frightened me.

The doctors wanted me to start using my new lungs by myself so it was decided that I should come off of the ventilator and try to breathe without any help, but apparently I really struggled with this and although I don't really remember clearly what happened next, I woke and I had had a tracheotomy, which is a tube that is inserted in to the neck, so I would be able to breathe more easily. This procedure was carried out in my Critical Care bay. I must have been put out for a short time for this to have taken place. I was really affected by this happening because I do get claustrophobic and having a trachy made me feel trapped.

Nighttime was the worst time for me. I was getting really hot although my bay was cool, but with all of the equipment working and all of the noises I was panicking, and my breathing was all over the place. Frederico, one of my many wonderful nurses, would see me struggling and come over and calm me, and breathe with me and tell me to relax, telling me that I was getting enough oxygen. Because I could not talk, I used to tap my fingers on my bed rails to get attention, and then I would try to mouth what I wanted and if that didn't work sometimes the nurses would get a pad of paper and a pen together with a sheet of letters and go along the letters pointing in turn until I nodded at the right one, it worked but it was a long job to create a sentence.

The first two nights I couldn't sleep and every time I closed my eyes, after a couple of minutes I would panic and have to open them again. My nurses used to plead with me to relax and get some sleep, but even though I was still very weak and dog tired I just could not give in and sleep. Another thing, at the entrance to my bay above the doorway was a digital wall clock and it had a black case with red numbers telling the time, and because of the position of me on my bed I could not help but look at it every time my eyes opened. It seemed to make the nights so long, watching almost every minute go by one by one. In the end I think I became so tired that after giving myself a good talking to and telling myself to get a grip I did finally manage to start getting a few hours sleep at night.

One of my nurses used to encourage me to do a few exercises and he used to help me by holding my legs up and pushing against me while I tried to push forward and the same with my arms. I really liked this, and it used to help me with my frame of mind.

Another thing the nurses used to do for me was to wash my face with cold water; I could have easily had this done nonstop because I used to get so hot. Jackie and Sonya used to do this for me as well when they visited and I must have been a pain in the neck for them because I used to keep mouthing "one more time" to them and I used to love seeing them laugh because they knew how crafty I was. They also used to give me some lovely feet and lower leg massages that really used to relax me.

When you are in my position, and you are totally reliant on the nurses for everything you learn very quickly to overcome any embarrassment and when you see them all in action together, like a team, it is a very emotional thing and something that I will never forget. They are wonderful people, all of them.

One morning, I think it was just after the doctors' rounds, a lady with a white uniform came in to see me. She said "hello Stephen my name is Annie and I am one of the physiotherapist's here, and we are going to try and get you to have a cough this morning, to help keep your new lungs clear".

Well, I wondered why Annie had said she was sorry about this before she had done anything but before I knew it she had inserted a tube into my trachy and pushed it in further until I almost erupted with the need to cough, which is what I did even though it was so uncomfortable. This was all over probably in about one or two minutes, but it felt like hours to me and I think this happened at least five or six times while I still had my trachy in. The tube was used to suck out any mucus that was freed when I coughed, and then during my stay in critical care I would regularly have what they called a suction, I could request one any time I felt that I had a build-up on my chest.

By this time, I was having regular visits to my bay from my three consultants who I have been under since I was first referred to Papworth. They are Doctor J Parmar, Doctor D Thomas and Doctor C Patterson, all of whom are not only truly wonderful doctors but I feel as though I can talk to them at ease about anything that concerns me about my transplant and, indeed, anything else on my mind. The same can be said about all of the transplant nurses.

During the day I remember that I used to get really hot, and when I asked one of my nurses for a face wash she said "how about if I get a pillow case and put some ice in it and wrap it around your neck and shoulders". I said "that would be lovely" so she went and got this done and it was a fantastic feeling to have this fresh ice cool wrap around my neck and shoulders, to help keep me cool. Nothing is too much trouble for these amazing critical care nurses.

One morning my critical care nurse had a young trainee with her, she was a lovely person and she was allowed to ask me if I would like her to give me a shave. Well, because I hadn't had a shave for about eight or nine days my stubble was quite thick and it was very difficult for her to move the shaver around my face, and there were a couple of times that I really winced inside when the shaver caught my stubble wrong. Still I told her thank you for helping me and that she had done a lovely job, she just smiled and when she put some cream on my face after I think she was pleased. After all, this is how these young nurses learn their trade.

The next big thing for me was asking if the catheter, which was in my rear, could be removed because I really felt the urge to push and go to the toilet like normal. This didn't take long and once it was done, I remember thinking to myself that was another little bridge crossed, one more step closer to normality again. The catheter in my front wasn't so bad, and stayed in place until I was ready to go to North 5, which is the ward I was on after critical care, but it was a relief when it did come out because that meant I was back to normal for my toilet needs. I have to tell you that using a bed pan when you cannot hardly move yourself is very difficult, and the first few times I found it almost embarrassing, because once I had finished going to the toilet the staff would come in and roll me over so that one of the nurses could clean me, and they had to stay in position whilst holding me, otherwise I would have just rolled back because I had no strength to support myself. I soon relaxed and accepted that these wonderful nurses are there totally for you, and it's just work for them, and they know the feelings that you are going through at times like this. My admiration and respect for these nurses is complete and total.

Another thing I would like to share with you is something that I usually try to avoid, television adverts. Let me explain, in the afternoons on critical care I would sometimes have the telly on, and there was an advert that really got to me. It was a Lloyds Bank commercial which showed a young black horse being looked after by an adult black horse, almost guarded and guided, with the words "no matter what you're going through, I'll look after you" with some lovely music in the background. This really struck a chord with me, because to me I was the little black horse, and Royal Papworth Hospital and the staff were the big black horse guiding and looking after me. Silly isn't it, how sometimes things affect you emotionally.

My medications were all given to me through my NG tube (in my nose), except my Adoport which is one of my main anti immunosuppressant's. That was placed under my tongue and because I was not allowed any fluids to drink it just used to dissolve, the nurse then used to pump my other drug's into my NG tube mixed with cold water. When the cold water went into my stomach it used to feel lovely. The nurse used to smile at me and say, "that cold water feels nice doesn't it?" and I just smiled back and nodded my head.

It is strange the things I used to notice whilst I was laid static in my bed, especially at night when I couldn't sleep very well. From my bay, directly opposite my doors, I could see the staffroom door, where all the nurses would keep their food and drink, etc. It was a door that had a security lock system and a glass panel in it so I could see into the room and I used to watch as they punched their numbers in and then go in and collect their food and drink. This used to make me then fantasise about food and drink, because I wasn't allowed any, and I just used to think "oh you lucky, lucky people!" To be able to just have what you want, when you want seemed like a million miles away for me. I made a promise to myself that never again would I take for granted even a glass of just plain water, although most of my thoughts were about ice cream, fresh fruit and a cold pint of Guinness.

There were other times whilst I was in critical care that I remember different things happening. One night, I think it was only about two or three days after I had been brought out of my coma, I was just led in bed trying to relax because at this time I was having trouble sleeping, the lights were all turned down, it must have been about midnight and it was relatively quiet for the critical care ward when all of a sudden there was a commotion going on in one of the bay's along from my bay. I don't know weather it was the drugs or whatever, but it sounded like an older lady who suddenly started to shout at the staff, using really bad language, asking for a particular nurse that she wanted but who was off duty at the time. Well, you should have heard it, she was shouting "get me Colin, I only want Colin", but when the nurses tried to reason with her and tell her that Colin was not on Duty, and in bed, she went into a frenzy, shouting really loudly "F..K off, don't lie to me, get me F.....G Colin, I only want him and nobody else will do". This must have gone on for about five or six minutes, the lady shouting and swearing and in the end I think they did ring Colin and he came to the ward to placate the lady, and then things calmed down, but I couldn't believe what I had just heard!

On another occasion it was early evening, Jackie and I were in my bay when we heard an alarm which I had not heard before. The noise was scary, we knew straight away that it was something serious because all of a sudden about six or seven nurses and Doctors were running down the corridor, I think one of them was pushing a crash trolly, then my nurse, Frederico, calmly pulled the curtain's across the doors and when we asked him what was going on, he said it was something like a code red, where a patient had taken a turn for the worse and immediate emergency action was needed to try to keep the patient alive. Well, you can only imagine what was going on in my mind at that time, hoping that the person was going to be OK, and thinking I hope that isn't going to happen to me. It is in times like that, you can really see just how much pressure the nurses and doctors are under, and how quickly they have to act, and the efficient and calm way in which they go about doing their job. The thing is, because of the nature of this hospital, you know that Papworth is a life and death situation hospital, and unfortunately not everyone makes it.

In the evenings whilst I was on critical care, Jackie would have to go, usually between 7.30–8.00pm, so I used to try and rest and relax and prepare myself mentally for the night ahead once she had gone. Sometimes I might watch a bit of telly, or maybe I would try to read a book but I was having trouble with my concentration at this time and couldn't really last very long without closing my eyes, but I tried. Later in the evening, usually about 10pm, one of the nurses would come into my bay and ask me if I would like a wash, and of course I used to nod yes please. When she had got everything that she needed to wash me, she used to ask me would you like me to use your Lynx to wash you and I again nodded yes please. These nurses are so lovely, she would wash me with warm water and of course my Lynx, which used to smell so nice to me, and then dry me off with a fluffy towel. This used to really help relax me and put me in a good frame of mind, so I could at least wind down and rest, even if it wasn't full sleep.

Once I had settled down, after maybe four to five days I remember that every day at around 10.00am a lady would come along to each bay pushing the coffee and tea trolley and would look into each bay and ask if you wanted anything. I used to make her laugh because I just nodded my head to everything even though she knew that I could have nothing. This really made me feel quite good inside, just the fact of putting a smile on someone's face. It is true that the more you are denied anything the stronger the desire to have it fills you.

Stuart and Sonya were by now having to go home for work and resume normal life, so Jackie's cousin Trish used to come up and stay with her and visit me during the week. We were so lucky because a friend of a friend had a lovely riverside apartment in Cambridge and he kindly let my family stay there free of charge, it was only about 15 minutes from Papworth. Such a kind thing to do, I will be eternally grateful to Rob for his generosity.

After about 10 to 12 days the doctors wanted me moved into a wheelchair, so that I was sitting upright to help with my lung function, so the team of physios came and started to put these harness type things around my body to lift me up with the lifts that are in each bay. Well, because I had no strength at all my body just seemed to crumple up, I could only just hold my head in place but they managed to sit me in the chair and prop me up with pillows then they turned me so that I could look out of the window which was behind my bed. This was the first time I had seen the outside world for about 12 days. It was grey looking and it was raining, but I could see people walking, cycling and driving cars, going about their everyday lives. I thought I can't wait to be able to do that again. I had only been sitting there for about 20 minutes before I asked to be put back in my bed because the pain at the base of my spine was so bad as I had been led down up until this point. This happened quite a few times and I was able to stay out longer each time, which pleased the doctors.

As the days passed the nurses started to take some of the dressings off and remove stitches which made me really think I was well on the way to recovery. Also they put in what they called a talking trachy which was fitted into the place where my trachy was done and this enabled me to talk, or should I say whisper sort of loudly, but at least I could now communicate through speech and this felt fantastic to me.

It's funny sometimes how coincidence happens; one morning I was talking (whispering) to Frederico, my nurse, and he said to me that he had worked at Salisbury District Hospital which is about a quarter of a mile away from where I live, and that he had rented a flat in Exeter Street, opposite a hotel come restaurant called the Chapter House. I said to him really, my oldest grandson Reece lives there now, in the top flat. Frederico said he could not believe that the flat was the same one he used to rent. Amazing isn't it that here I was 150 miles away from home, in Critical Care with my nurse Frederico who had lived in the same flat that my grandson Reece was now living in!

One morning my consultant, Dr Jas Parmar, came into my room and said "Stephen, today you are going to have your first bronchoscope so we can see how your new lungs are looking." I knew what this would involve so I asked him if I would be put out for this and he said "well, you can be sedated if you wish, but I think you are the type of man who would like to see your new lungs for yourself and they will be shown on the screen with the camera probe which will be inserted into your trachy then go down into your lungs so we can see how they are doing. Don't worry, I can spray your throat so it will be completely numb, and you won't feel anything". Well, how could I say no? Doctor Parmar and his team brought the equipment in by my bed and he came over and took out the talking trachy then sprayed about five or six times into my throat until it was completely numb. The screen was just in front of me. Doctor Parmar was by my side and he started to insert the probe into my throat and then on down until he reached my lungs, all of which I could see on the screen. It was unbelievable, he was pointing out to me all the different parts and showing where Mr Tsui had joined my new lungs to my body, all totally pain free. When he had finished, he said "well done Stephen, it was worth it wasn't it?" I just nodded yes, it was amazing. He said that everything looked fine.

The days were now starting to get a little easier for me. I was coping better with things and my mood was more positive, I was thinking nice thoughts like imagining walking on a beach and hearing the sea, or hearing birds singing and seeing family and friends again.

I was also now allowed to sip cold water from a plastic cup but I had to promise to spit it back out once I had rinsed my mouth, which of course I did, but it was heavenly to be able to feel cold water in my mouth again.

Then, at last, came the day that my trachy was coming out. I knew that this was coming because there had been talk between the Doctors about getting me out of Critical Care and moved up to Level 5 North, which is the surgical ward where I would stay until I was discharged. The procedure was done in my bay, it was pain free and quite quick and at the end of it a small round plaster was put over the small hole in my throat. Great, I thought, another little step back towards normality and I didn't really notice how well I was breathing now without the need for extra oxygen.

However, after a day or so the Doctors soon realised that I had some throat damage caused by the trachy, so a team of speech and nutrition specialists became involved to monitor when I would be able to eat and drink. I had to have a test to see what was happening in my throat. Once this was done, I was given several different throat exercises to do over the weekend before I could leave Critical Care. Frederico and my other nurses helped me complete all of my exercises over the weekend. Nothing was too much trouble for them.

I had a lovely surprise in the afternoon on Sunday 13th October, when a staff nurse came into my bay and said she was going to get a wheelchair, and with Frederico's help get me in it and take me out of the ward for a walk outside for some fresh air. By now I was able to support myself a little better and with a blanket wrapped around me, and with Frederico carrying an emergency pack, off we went. It seemed really strange to me, to feel motion again, looking around and seeing the world in action. We ended up going to different parts of the hospital and when we went outside by the duck pond I could really feel the chilly fresh air on my face, and how nice it felt to breath cold air and not have to cough. I looked up at the sky and thought, well here we are, I'm looking at you again and we've made it this far. It felt wonderful to be outside for the first time since my transplant, my spirit lifted and my feelgood factor was off the scale.

It was a special weekend for me as Sonya and Stuart visited and Sonya brought my two youngest grandsons, Louie and Finley, up to see me. A lovely surprise.

When the doctors came round on Monday morning, 14th October, it was my 20th and last day in Critical Care. I was on my way to North 5, the next step of my journey was about to start. I didn't get a chance to thank all of the amazing, wonderful family of nurses and doctors on Critical Care, but my life has been saved by them; somehow thank you doesn't seem enough but I'm sure they know what I mean.

First sense of normal life – meal out with family for Stuart's birthday

Stuart and Sonya

Me with my wife Jackie

My three grandsons, Finlay, Louie and Reece

With Willow

On the Isle of Wight - Within the last 5 months

TUESDAY OCTOBER 15th, 2019

Level 5 North

As I was being pushed along on my way to North 5 it suddenly hit me how relatively quiet things were compared to the constant hustle and bustle in Critical Care. I was taken to my room and slid over onto the bed, the nurses were very careful because I was still nil by mouth and my NG tube was still in place. When all was done, I laid back and had a good look around my room. It was lovely, a nice window with views over the medial campus, my own bathroom, a nice armchair and a nice big telly all to myself.

Don't forget that this was the brand new Royal Papworth Hospital, it had only been opened by the Queen a couple of months ago and it is a truly wonderful hospital. As I settled down to sleep on the first night on North 5 I found it difficult to drop off, my mind constantly thinking back to my time on Critical Care, the noises, the alarms and busy staff yet here in my room now it was almost silent, I couldn't believe the difference.

The next morning, once I had been washed and dressed, one of the transplant nurses came in and had in her hand a blue book. She told me it was for me to write down my medications, weight, temperature and lung function each day. Luckily Jackie was with me so the nurse showed us both what to do. It was a daunting thing to start with but after a few days we got used to it. The little blue book is now referred to as the Papworth Bible and I have to carry it with me at all times in case of an emergency, and the information in the book is everything that another doctor or hospital would need to know. At this point I must have been on about 10 different medications, with various dosages and times to take them so it took a while to get things right.

After going through all of my medications, Monika, one of the transplant specialist nurses, sat down with Jackie and I and began to go through all of my dietary needs. There are a lot of foods and drink that I am now not allowed to have, such as, some soft cheeses, some yogurts, buffet foods, all meats have to be well cooked, my egg's all have to be hard, (no more soft fried, poached or boiled eggs) I could have cried, but it's a small price to pay. Also I'm not allowed grapefruit juice again, or real ale from the handpump, though bottles are OK as long as the ale is pasteurised, and if we go out for a meal my food has to be freshly cooked. There are many things to learn about, but Papworth are always there to help and guide you along the way. Monika also informed me that I am not to be uncovered in the sun anymore, because of my medication, so no more nice brown tan for me! Never mind, slowly but surely all of the special things that your life has now to follow fall into place.

The next thing that happened was about mid morning when a couple of physios came into my room and told me they would like me to try and stand, with their help of course, so they moved me to the side of the bed, one either side of me and whilst holding me said that they were going to rock me forward and then back, and on the third time forward they wanted me to try and stand. I never realised until that moment just how weak my legs were after 20 days of lying down in Critical Care. I couldn't hold myself up without their help. This got easier over the next few days, and then I started using a walking frame to try a few steps at a time. In the end I was walking about 10 to 15 metres at a time, the physios loved that, I suppose my training history helped me because I was very determined.

By now I could get off of my bed without help and use my walker to go to the bathroom, etc. This was a real turning point for me; I really was starting to feel like the old me. Also in my room there was an exercise bike which I could use anytime I liked.

One of the nurses came into my room and said

"Hello Stephen, I'm going to make you a teddy".

"What's that then?"

"It's a folded-up pillow of sorts and you use it to put to your chest and hold it when you cough so that it doesn't hurt so much."

Such a simple thing but it really worked. Because I had throat damage the nurses from the speech and nutrition department came to test my ability to eat and drink. This involved putting a small camera probe with a light on the end of it into my nose and down into my throat. I was given a tiny amount of water which I had to swallow, so the camera would then show how my throat was working. This was the first time I had swallowed anything for about three and a half weeks and it felt great. I then had to swallow a slightly thicker liquid with a dye in it so the team could see what wasn't working in my throat properly. The final test was for me to swallow some yoghurt because it is even thicker and I can tell you the moment that yoghurt went on my tongue, the taste was like the best thing I have ever tasted in my life! At the end of the tests the team agreed I could from now on have small sips of water to drink, but no solid food. Another test was planned for later in the week.

I was doing more work with the physios now, slowly walking unaided down to the gym where we were doing all sorts of exercise. It felt great to be able to work my body again. In the afternoons I would usually rest, and it was while I was doing this that I noticed a man continually walking around the ward corridors. When you are able the staff encourage you to do this and I thought, look at that man, doing the best he can for himself, I want to do that when I'm able to. He gave me great incentive. He was in the room next to me and when I did start to walk around the ward I bumped into him and told him that he had inspired me, which made him laugh, but he was really pleased and we became good friends, his name's David.

One day there was a knock on my door, it was a volunteer who worked at the hospital. He said to me that if I was able, would I like to walk down to the communal room to have my lunch, where I could also meet and talk with other patients. I said yes, I would, and David said the same, so we used to walk down together and spend an hour or so having lunch and chatting. On another occasion I was sitting up in bed drowsing when a tap on the door sort of woke me. It was a gentleman volunteer who went around to patients asking if they would like to have some company and talk for a while, which we did. It was very interesting how soon you find common ground with a stranger. He saw me a couple of times and I thought how kind it was of people to give up their time for others, but he said to me how much he enjoyed doing it.

It was now four days since my throat test and today (Friday, October 18th) was test day again. The girls from the speech unit came in with their equipment and the same procedure took place, us all watching the screen. Jackie was with me as well and at the end of it they decided that it would be okay for me to start having a little solid food. Great I thought, I hadn't eaten any solid food for nearly a month now, so I couldn't wait to get started and I knew that my weight had dropped about 10kg over that time. The nurse brought me a menu and I chose soup with a roll and then a light sandwich. It was lovely to taste food again, but I had trouble moving my tongue around my mouth because I hadn't used it for the last month, and because it's a muscle it needed exercise! Never mind, I managed and the bonus about my condition was that I had an extra menu to choose from to help me gain weight and that included things like chocolate bars, crisps, sausage rolls, ice cream and cheese and biscuits. Lovely stuff, but I was only allowed three items a day.

Later that afternoon I had a surprise visitor to my room. It was Mr Steven Tsui, the surgeon who performed my transplant. It was wonderful to see him and thank him for saving my life. He sat with Jackie and we talked about things. He told me how near to the edge I was and how I nearly died on the operating table, but he was so pleased that I was now doing quite well. He is a lovely down to earth man and easy to talk to but so much depends on men like him and they just seem to take it all in their stride. I shook his hand and Jackie took a photo of us together.

I found that meeting incredibly emotional. By now I was getting used to the daily routine and was doing well and feeling more and more that I could cope with much more, and I was feeling more independent. I really enjoyed the visits from my sister Diane and her husband Barry, and from my brother Rob and his wife Liz, also my friends Tony, Andy, Sharon and Chris, my mate Brian and Sandra from work, the two Matty's from work and Alan, all who had driven 150 miles to see me, it meant a lot to me to see them all. Jackie's cousin Kim and her husband Jeff, who only live about two miles from Papworth used to visit and were so kind to pick Jackie up and take her back to the apartment most evenings. It is so nice to have good people around you at a time like this.

By this time I was now allowed off of the ward and I really enjoyed going down to the cafe and having coffee with Jackie and whoever was visiting at the time, all of these little things help you so much in so many ways, just the feeling of normality gradually coming back. On 26th October it was my son Stuart's birthday and as a treat I was allowed to go out to a restaurant with him, Jackie and Sonya for lunch. We went to Bella Italia and it was a lovely afternoon because after we'd eaten, they took me back to see the apartment where they had been staying and a lovely surprise awaited me there. Jackie had gone out and bought a big tub of ice cream and some fresh fruit, one of my fantasies when I was in Critical Care, and we sat down and enjoyed my treat before going back to hospital. Another special time for me was a phone call to my Dad, Henry, who was unable to travel all the way to see me but I know how much it meant to him for us to speak so I really enjoyed talking to him, although it was emotional because he was so far away.

I knew that the doctors were now talking about me going home but before that happened I had to have a lung biopsy, which I had been told about but was not really looking forward to because this involved being taken to a small theatre and then having spray in my throat to numb any feeling and a mild sedative to help me relax while the operation took place. I had a mouth guard with a hole in the centre, into which the doctor would feed small pincers and push them down to the lungs then cut several small pieces for examination. It sounds painful and I thought it would be, but in reality I was almost asleep during the procedure and hardly felt a thing. Back up on the ward I felt a bit groggy, perhaps because of the sedative and just wanted to be alone. I had an episode like this when I was in Critical Care, Jackie and Sonya came to visit me and I just brushed them away, I don't really remember this but it upset them and I felt really bad when they told me. The nurse said this happens with quite a few patients. It must be all of the drugs.

My biopsy results showed a slight rejection. It sounds scary but it is treated with drugs and I had to have intravenous prednisolone for two days. My next tests showed that everything was fine, and I was set to go home the next day, which was November 1st, my Mum's birthday. I think it was meant to be. It seemed really strange, Jackie and I getting all of my stuff together for the journey home, it just didn't seem real. Our friend Chris was coming to take us home and after thanking all of the nurses on North 5 and picking up all of my drugs we finally walked out of Papworth and back into normal life. I felt a little scared if I'm honest, but I knew that at any time I could ring Papworth for support and advice. I must just say that on the Friday evening before I left hospital Mr Tsui came to see me. He was really pleased at how well I was, and he said to me "Stephen, what you need to do now is go home, get yourself fit and stay well, enjoy your family and do the things that you have talked about, you are a good hard working man and now is the time to do those things." Those words meant a lot to me and Jackie.

After getting home and settling in I must admit I did feel very vulnerable, you do get used to having all the staff with you at the hospital but that feeling soon went and I have the comforting thought in the back of my mind that Papworth is and will be there for me for the rest of my life. It's almost like when I go there for my clinic appointments I'm going back to friends and the family of nurses, doctors and all the staff who were there for me, it's very reassuring to have that feeling. After I had been home for the first few days, then weeks, and then a couple of months, over this time I thought more and more about what I had been through, that it's all been real, such a huge thing in mine and my family's lives.

I must write a few words to tell you about how much my cat Willow has helped in my recovery at home. Jackie and I have two cats, Nala, who is more Jackie's cat, and Willow, who is more my cat. I think that cats can sense sometimes when you are struggling with things, and the number of times Willow has just appeared on my shoulder when I'm sat watching telly, or in a quiet moment I couldn't begin to guess. She will gently nudge me for a kiss or attention and then lay so that I can put my arm around her and she will bury her head into my shoulder, and somehow her purr's are so comforting and relaxing, it really is like therapy.

I didn't have much time when I was in hospital to give proper thought about the wonderful, kind person who saved my life – my donor. The truth is as I write this story, I myself do not know anything about my donor, but I can tell you that I get very emotional when I'm in a quiet moment of reflection, just sat watching the telly or listening to music, something triggers my thoughts and I think deeply about my donor, did he or she have a family, how old he or she was and what happened to him or her. I hope one day I will know the answers to some of these questions, but Papworth will help me with this once the time is right and maybe I can write my donor's family a letter to thank them for their precious gift. I do feel in my life now that I'm living for the two of us, and I have made a silent promise that I will try my best to live a healthy, good life for the rest of my life to honour my donor. I think that anyone who is on a live transplant list doesn't wish any person any harm, it's just that when that call comes, you know that the person who is going to be your donor has wished for this to happen and should you be the one chosen, do all you can to help their wish come true. I treasure every day now that I have been given life again.

Before I sign off, I must also thank my consultant at Southampton General Hospital, Dr Sophie Fletcher, who referred me to Papworth where I had my transplant and where my story ends. Of course it doesn't ever really end, I will be going to Papworth for the rest of my life and my thanks to the Royal Papworth Hospital and the NHS knows no limits, thank you just doesn't seem enough but it's all I have.

THANK YOU.

This whole process has been hard on my family, watching me come through all of this but I am so lucky to have such a loving family, they were all together to support each other. My wife Jackie has been my rock throughout this, always there for me. I know that both of our lives have changed forever now, and I know that Jackie has to face things with me, but she never complains she just gets on with it, sometimes telling me off! I want her to know that I'm glad it's her by my side and that I love her and cherish her love for me.

I hope whoever reads this will enjoy it and understand my feelings and experiences of my transplant story. Thanks.

TUESDAY AUGUST 25th, 2020

Papworth

Today I am going to Papworth for a clinic appointment and I have some news for you about my donor. I can tell you that my donor was a lady in her mid fifties, and to know this filled me with so many emotions, the wondering and not knowing now filled with at least an image in my mind of maybe how my donor looked, although of course I may never really know. I want to say thank you to her so much, I wish that I could hug her and tell her of all the things that her gift of life has meant to myself, my family and friends, and how because of her my dreams are still alive because without her gift my dreams would be gone along with my life itself. I am really struggling to find and write the words of thanks to my donor and her family, its like asking someone to say the biggest number they could ever think of, but maybe somewhere, somehow, my donor knows that what she wanted to happen has resulted in what I can only call a miracle. I think about her and thank her every day. Organ donors such as my donor, are the people that make stories such as mine possible.

IN CLOSING

There are some thoughts that I would like to share with everyone, but especially those people who are waiting on, or are about to go onto a live transplant list. I know some of the thoughts that will be going through your minds, all the things that can go wrong, how long will I live after my transplant, all the things I have to do afterwards, what if I don't wake up again?

There are these thoughts plus another hundred or more questions you will ask yourself, but if I can try and reassure you that over time while you are waiting you will slowly come to terms with what you are going to go through. The love of a good family and friends also helps a lot. Once you are through your transplant and back at home there are times that you will learn things about yourself that may surprise you. As I got better and stronger the weeks seemed to fly by, and often I would be sat watching telly with Jackie when all of a sudden it would hit me just what had happened over the last couple of months. I used to say to myself in my mind "I've had a double lung transplant" almost in disbelief, then the realisation that it all did happen, and how far we've all come since my transplant. Also, when listening to music I do get very emotional when certain tracks are played, you can't help it, the moment just grabs you and so many thoughts go through your mind. I feel as though I was reborn on the 26th September 2019 and I will celebrate this day as another birthday that I share with my wonderful unknown donor. By the way, my own birthday is November 19th which I share with my middle grandson Louie, so I really don't have a birthday all to myself!

Well there we are, I'm all done but before I finish I would like to wish anyone about to go through their own transplant story my love and best wishes, and I hope your story turns out like mine.

Best wishes
Stephen

ACKNOWLEDGEMENTS

This book would not have been possible without the support and encouragement of my wife, Jackie, and my children Sonya and Stuart. Also, thanks to Tony Read for his support with my book.

Christine Harding – for writing the foreword

Mr Steven Tsui and his team at Royal Papworth

The NHS and all the Staff at the Royal Papworth Hospital

Dr S. Fletcher – Southampton General Hospital

Dr Jas Parmar – Royal Papworth Hospital

Dr D. Thomas – Royal Papworth Hospital

Dr C. Patterson – Royal Papworth Hospital

Dan – the ambulance man

Tony Read, Andy Downs, Roger Brocksom, Mike Robinson, Paul Sergeant, Chris Addison, Chris Pearse, Barry & Di – for all of the lifts to and from Papworth

Rob Hancox – for the kind use of his flat

Jeff & Kim – for the lifts in Cambridge

Chris & Sharon McDonald and Chris and Andrea Pearse – for all the shopping trips

All of my family, work mates and friends.

Thanks also to Duncan Potter and Paul Beaney of Riverside Publishing solutions for their help, advice and support in the production of this book.

www.riversidepublishingsolutions.com